The Very Basic Series:
Technology Made Easy

Get Plugged In
A Beginner's Guide for
How to Use a Computer and Go Online

3rd Edition

Author
JoAnna S. Sanfeld

This product is for use with
most computer operating systems
such as
Windows® operating system or Mac OS®

This publication is designed to provide basic information with regard to the
subject matter covered. It is sold with the understanding that the author and
publisher are not engaged in rendering advice or instruction related to specific
technology that would require familiarity and/or use of the features and
specifications of many or all makes and models of technological products.
Instead, this publication is intended to provide general information related to
how to use a computer and the Internet for personal use. The reader should
always rely on manufacturer user manuals and other documentation available for
specific computers and other computer related products. Any information in this
book that conflicts with such manuals or other documentation, the manufacturer
documentation shall take precedence. This publication is sold with the
understanding that the publisher is not engaged in rendering legal, accounting, or

other professional advice. If expert assistance is required, the services of a competent professional person should be sought.

Dedication

To my husband,
who inspired me to write this book

_____

Introduction

Congratulations! You have decided to learn about how to use a computer and how to use the Internet! This book will help you build these skills. If you are familiar with *The Very Basics Series*[©], then you know that it is intended to help make technology easy. This book is part of the *The Very Basics Series*[©] and is for anyone that wants to learn the very basics about using a computer, for personal use, and how to use the Internet.

If you just acquired a computer, where do you start? What do you do when you take it out of the box? How do you connect cables and cords to the computer? What do the keys on a computer keyboard actually do? How do I use the Internet? If these are some of the basic questions that you want answered, this self-help book is for you.

The other good news is that this book does not use complicated computer  terminology. This book begins with the assumption that you have minimal or no knowledge about using a computer or the Internet. Most computer training available today is for someone with some computer knowledge. This may not have been the intention of existing computer training, but research has shown that computer training on the market today is too difficult to follow and understand for many beginners because the training utilizes computer terms or moves too fast for many beginners. Such training many times assumes you know common computer terminology when you may not. This book breaks through this traditionally standard way of teaching computer skills by first taking learners to the basics of computer use training.

The information in this book is not intended to replace information in the manufacturer or other documentation for your computer. Please rely on the manufacturers' documentation if anything in this book conflicts with that documentation.

Also, this book provides information regarding how to use a computer for personal use and is useful information unrelated to whether you use a PC or Mac.

So sit back and trust that you finally found the right self-help book to get you started computing! So let's get started!

Following this introduction is the table of contents for this book. Use the table of contents when you want to jump to a specific topic. However, if you have no or little experience using a personal computer, then you will likely read this book in the order it is presented. Oh, just one reminder – don't forget these basic rules which are the most important:

1. Pat yourself on the back often! You have decided to learn more about computers and the Internet, right? Congratulations! You should be proud of yourself! Go ahead – celebrate now! You should also take time to pat yourself on the back every time you learn something new, no matter how small the step or new insight that you have gained – like, I learned today how to turn the computer on and off safely! That deserves a pat – do it often as you learn new computer skills!

2. Be patient! You may get frustrated from time to time, but with this book, your frustrations will not only be minimized but may totally go away! We make the basics of using a personal computer and the Internet so easy to follow, that you will probably zoom through this book! If you do get frustrated, however, it's okay! It will be short-lived. Just don't let it sidetrack you and give up all together. Just take a break and come back to it later. Trust me, you can do this.

3. This has nothing to do with intelligence! It doesn't matter how smart you are or are not. Everyone has to take time to gain computer skills to

use a computer. Then, it's a matter of how often we use newly learned skills that determines how much of it that we retain. It's like learning to ride a bicycle, right? It takes a little practice but once you learn, it becomes more intuitive.

4.   Have fun! Learning computers is fun – it really is! You will be delighted with how much you learn, and how easy you learned it, as you progress through this book.

Now, go to the table of contents to decide if you want to start at the beginning of the book or somewhere else that will more quickly meet your needs.

To learn how to use specific computer programs (like word processing, e-mail, etc.), see other books that are part of *The Very Basic Series*[©].

Table of Contents

Lesson 1

What Can I Do With a Personal Computer?

 Computers can be used for many things. Perhaps this is why you are interested in learning how to use one. It's also exciting to learn new things. What's exciting about learning to use a computer is that it will open up an entire new world for you! Computers are used today for personal and business purposes. This book focuses on how to use a computer for personal use.

It isn't possible to show you how to do everything there is to do on a computer for personal use in one book. This is because there are literally millions, of computer programs that have a variety of purposes. This book starts with the basics that allow you to get started using a computer and the Internet.

Let's start with a few things that most people want to learn to use a computer.

➢ **Things I can do with a computer offline**

Following is a list of example things you can do with a computer offline – this refers to using the computer **without** being connected to the Internet:

- Read and write letters or other documents – and edit them easily (using a word-processing program).

- Have a program that does math functions for you (using a spreadsheet program).

- Make calendar or address book entries that are easier to maintain than writing it down (using a calendar or address book program).

- Keep to-do or other task lists (using a program that does these things).

- Draw and design almost anything (using programs that allow you to draw and design)

To do many of these things, you would need to have programs on your computer that allow you to do them. Most computers come with some basic programs that allow you to do the above tasks.

➢ **Things I can do with a computer online (using the Internet)**

When you use the Internet, your world really begins to open up more so regarding what you can do with a computer. Here is a list of just a few examples of things you can do on the Internet:

- Communicate with family and friends, such as using e-mail
- Check, buy and sell stock online or make other investments
- Check winning lottery ticket number!
- Shop for almost anything
- Check your checking or savings account activity or balances
- Play games or compete with other playing games online

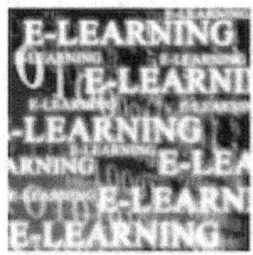

- Take educational courses
- Make appointments
- Find answers to health questions
- Find a place to go to for vacation
- Get discounts not available anywhere else
- Research or learn about anything!
- Download and read a book immediately

- Buy and sell almost anything
- Find driving directions or a location on a map
- Write and distribute a newsletter on line – without stamps!
- Fill prescriptions
- Pay your bills
- Apply for credit cards and find the best credit rates
- Plan and book your next fishing trip
- Buy programs for your computer and download some free applications and updates
- Turn your information into graphs
- See what's playing at theatres, order tickets on line, even make your own movies
- Research your family history or find family members and friends
- Purchase and download books
- Get lots of free stuff
- Take advantage of online discounts that are not available except on the Internet
- Visit with family and friends anywhere, in real time if you would like, and be able to see each other while you are talking!
- Book travel and receive confirmations of booked travel
- Download music

The list could literally be endless! You basically will gain access to the world!

Lesson 2

Personal Computer Options

> **Types of computers for personal use**

Computers are machines that 'compute' for you. Computers typically have small 'chips' that hold the computer's operating system and stores your computer programs and data that you save on your computer. Personal computers come in a variety of options, including those that sit on your desk, sit on your lap, or can easily fit in your hand.

In this book, we will be focusing on two basic types of personal computers: a desktop computer and laptop (also called a notebook) computer.

> **Desktop computers**

A desktop computer typically sits on a desk. This is where it originally got its name. The image here is representative of a desktop computer.

A desktop computer is convenient if you expect to use it in one location most of the time. All of these components in the image don't need to sit on the desk. For example, the component called a "tower" is typically sitting on the floor near the desk.

Desktop Computer

The benefits of a desktop computer, compared to a laptop, are that you typically have a larger display monitor and keyboard in most cases. These can help with ease of use if you are new to using a computer. This isn't particularly a concern for some new computer users, who prefer the benefits of a laptop that are covered next.

The components of a desktop computer will be covered in more detail in the next lesson.

➤ Laptop (notebook) computers

The laptop computer is smaller than a desktop, is one piece and folds shut. It is referred to as a laptop computer because many people set the computer on their laps when using it. Laptops are also known as notebook computers because they are about the size of a notebook and open similar to a book. The image here is representative of a laptop computer.

Laptop Computer

A laptop computer may be your computer of choice if you want to be able to use it in multiple locations in your home, perhaps on your patio, and if you want to be able to take your computer with you when you travel. Optional computer bags for travel purposes are available. The portability of laptop computers is the reason most people buy and use them. Laptops today come in many sizes with display sizes available that are as large as desktop displays.

You can also connect other hardware to a laptop similar to a desktop computer, such as a mouse, external speakers, or a printer. Many laptop users do not connect a mouse and instead use the built in touch pad that serves the same functions as a mouse. All personal computers have speakers built into them but some people like external speakers as well. Printers and other computer components today can be connected wirelessly to your computer (this typically requires a wireless modem or similar component to do this).

The components of a laptop computer will be covered in more detail in the next lesson.

If you haven't purchased your computer yet and you are not sure whether to purchase a desktop or laptop computer, you may want to ask other computer owners that you know to find out why they prefer a desktop or laptop computer. This may help you with your purchase decision.

➢ **Which computer is best for me?**

If you don't already have your computer, you may be thinking through which computer is best for you – a desktop computer or a laptop computer. Hopefully, the description earlier in this book of both types of computers was helpful to you in making this decision. However, experience has shown that you may want to consider the following in making your purchase decision:

- **Cost** – At the time this book was published, feature-for-feature, desktop computers are less expensive than laptops. Some would say that this is paying for the convenience of the portability of a laptop computer. Keep in mind, however, that any computer you buy will be more expensive when additional features or capabilities are added to the computer, and can quickly become comparable in cost.

- **Computer Features** – What do you minimally need on a computer if you are a novice? Basically, you don't need a lot of bells and whistles on your computer. In other words, if you ask for the low-end computer of either the desktop or laptop, it should do everything (and more) that  you need. In making this decision, ask yourself what do you want to do with the computer? This is what the sales person in the store should ask you should ask you so they can direct you to the computer models that will serve your needs. There are not features or capabilities on a laptop computer that is not on a desktop computer or vice versa so features and capabilities should not impact your decision regarding whether to purchase a desktop or laptop computer. Yes, you may have different options to do similar tasks on these two computers, but the capabilities of both styles of computers are generally similar. An example is a mouse is typically utilized with a desktop and a touch pad or mouse can be used with a laptop to do similar functions.

- **Portability** – Will you want to use the computer in different locations in your house on a regular basis or do you believe you will be fine with using the computer in one location? You can move a desktop or laptop to different locations in your home, but a desktop is not intended to move frequently, as it is hard-wired and has larger components. A laptop actually only requires a power cord to function and can run on its battery without its power cord for periods of time. Another consideration is if you will want the flexibility to be able to take your computer with you when traveling. If this is the case, then you will want a laptop computer instead of a desktop. (This book does not address handheld computers but this is also an option for portability but not recommended for new computer users – you will graduate to a handheld soon enough!)

- **Screen Size** – It used to be that if you preferred a larger screen, that this was good reason to purchase a laptop. This is not particularly true anymore. Yes, there likely are some desktop monitors that have screens that are larger than you can get on a laptop computer. However, laptops today have up to 17" screens (perhaps larger) that are mass marketed that is comparable to many desktop computers.

- **Keyboards** – Typically, you will have more keyboard options with a desktop computer over a laptop. You can match up a variety of keyboards with desktops, many of which have a separate numbers keypad on the keyboard. Most laptops don't have the numbers keypad. If you know before your purchase that a numbers keypad is important to you, you will want to spend time looking at the keyboards of the computers you are considering for purchase. Additionally, some laptops have smaller keys that desktop keyboards. If the size of the keys are important to you, this will be a consideration for you. Today, however, there are also many laptops on the market that have similar size keys as that of desktops.

Lesson 3

I Have A Computer – Now What Do I Do?

➤ **Taking the computer out of the box and setup**

Congratulations! This is the fun part! (It's really not hard…) Whether you have a desktop or laptop computer will determine what you have to do to set up your computer.

Most new computers, and sometimes used ones, include a quick start guide, a setup guide, and other documentation with additional documentation available online on their web sites. It is highly recommended that you rely on these guides and other manufacturer documentation when setting up your computer and computer components. You will also want to rely on this documentation if it is necessary to load any operating systems or software programs onto your computer.

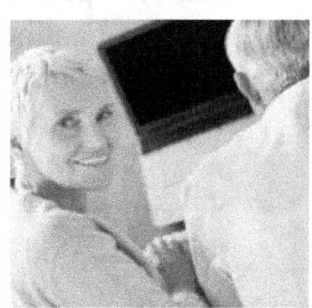

➤ **Computer components**

• **Major components of a desktop computer**

You can skip this section if you have a laptop computer.

The main parts of a desktop computer typically is a separate monitor (also called a display), keyboard, the motherboard and other internal components that are located in the tower, and a mouse. You may also have external speakers, a printer, or other pieces of computer hardware to connect to your computer.

There is an image of a representative desktop computer here with the parts of the computer labeled. Images of computer hardware in this book are only illustrative of typical layouts of computers and other computer hardware. However, your computer hardware or components may be arrange differently, look somewhat differently, or be a different color than as shown.

- **Major components of a laptop (notebook) computer**

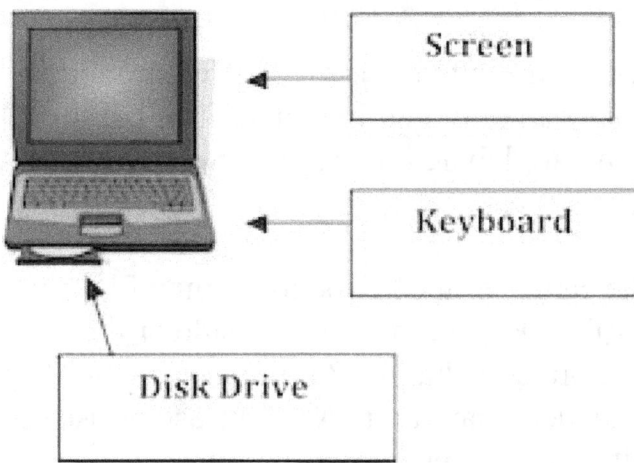

The laptop (or notebook computer) is smaller than a desktop, is one piece and folds shut. The laptop computer will look similar to the image here. Basically there is a keyboard, a screen, and a power cord. After your laptop is fully charged, you can use your laptop without the power cord, as the battery allows.

- **More detailed description of computer components**

  o **Monitor or display (the screen)**

  The monitor is the part of your computer that holds the computer display or screen. The display is where the output of what you do on the computer is "displayed." The quality of the output of what you do on the computer and how the display is laid out is largely controlled by the operating system. The display is available in different sizes for both the desktop and laptop computers.

  o **The keyboard**

  No, you don't need to be able to type to use your keyboard. Yes, you will do less 'hunting and pecking' on the keyboard if you know how to type. The letter keys

17

are laid out somewhat similar to the typewriter, but you also have extra keys on a computer keyboard that a typewriter does not have. You will do a lot of pecking with one finger for awhile if you aren't used to using a computer keyboard. That's okay. Don't get frustrated with it. You will learn to move about the keyboard better the more you use your computer. We will assume you can't type and have no computer keyboard experience for this discussion.

Let's talk about how your keyboard is arranged. No two different models of keyboards are exactly alike so we can only talk in generalities but the keys typically do the same thing and are labeled the same or very similarly.

The letter keys are generally in the center of the keyboard. You will have a row of numbers at the top of the keyboard or to one side or the other or both. It's the special function keys that need more explanation but we won't explain all the special keys that you may never use or use very seldom. If you need help with any of these, refer to your computer documentation. The special function keys that we are going to cover here are located in the same general place on all keyboards but not exactly. Some keyboards have special keys that other keyboards do not – don't worry about this. You will have all the keys you need on all keyboards.

Also, some keys on keyboards are multi-function – they do more than  one thing. For most of the multi-function keys, press and hold the SHIFT key first when you want to use a function on the top of any key. The only exceptions are the keys that are located across or near the top of your keyboard that are labeled with the letter F with a number (for example, F1, F2, F3…F12). These F keys are used in combination with the FUNCTION key (usually labeled FN for "Function"). Following are explanations of keys on your keyboard, where each key is typically located on a keyboard, and what each key usually does. You may also have some other special keys on your keyboard that may be specific to your keyboard.

The Keyboard Quick Reference Chart

Note: The keys described in this chart may be programmed on your computer do something differently than as shown here. Rely on manufacturer documentation for your keyboard for information regarding your keyboard.

The Key	Where its Typically Located	What the Key Does
ALT Key	Usually located at the bottom right of the keyboard. You may not have an ALT key on your keyboard.	Used in combination with other keys to do special functions
ARROW Keys	Usually located at bottom right of the keyboard	Will move you in the direction indicated on the key without deleting anything you move to or move over
BACKSPACE Key	Usually located on the right side of the keyboard toward the top	It goes back a space and will delete the character typed in the previous space
BREAK Key	Usually located in the top right area of the keyboard. You may not have a BREAK key.	Stops a function
CAPS LOCK Key	Usually on left side of the keyboard and	Press and release this key (don't need to

The Key	Where its Typically Located	What the Key Does
	there may be one on each side of your keyboard	hold). It's a toggle key until pressed again. When pressed, it locks the keyboard to all capital letters until pressed again.
COMMAND Key	This key is usually only on some computer keyboards and is typically located to the left and right of the space bar on your keyboard.	This key is used to do many special functions when used in combination with other keys.
CONTROL Key	There are usually 2 control keys with one located on each side of the keyboard	A control key is usually used in combination with another key to do special functions
DELETE Key	Usually located near the top right corner of the keyboard	Deletes what is after the cursor
END Key	Usually located at right side of key board	Moves the cursor or pointer to the end of a line, a page, or document
ENTER (Return) Key	Usually located at the right side of the keyboard and can be	Takes you down one line; using this key on web sites typically

The Key	Where its Typically Located	What the Key Does
	labeled "return" or "enter" or simply with a left arrow; it is typically a larger key since it is used often.	does the same thing as pressing the ENTER or OKAY key on the site
ESCAPE Key	Usually located in the top left corner of the keyboard.	Backs you out of a function or task that is running
FUNCTION Key	Usually located at the bottom left of the keyboard	This key is used in combination with the FUNCTION NUMBER keys to do special functions
FUNCTION NUMBER Keys	Located in a row along the top of the keyboard	These keys are usually used in combination with other specific keys to do special functions.
NUMBER PAD	Located on the right side of the keyboard	The keys on the number pad work the same as the numbers near the top of the keyboard; press the NUM LOCK key before using the number keys on the pad if you want to type several numbers
OPTION Key	This key is usually	This key is used in

The Key	Where its Typically Located	What the Key Does
	located on the left and right in the bottom row of the keyboard. This key is not needed or available on all keyboards.	combination with other keys to do special functions.
PAGE UP and PAGE DOWN Keys	Usually located at the top right corner of the keyboard	Moves your location up or down one page
PAUSE Key	Usually located in the top right area of the keyboard	Pauses a function; if the PAUSE is the top function of a key (as in this photo), you will need to press and hold the SHIFT key before pressing the PAUSE key
POWER Button	Usually located at the top center of the keyboard for laptops and on the tower for desktop computers	Turns the computer on
PRINT SCREEN Key	Usually located in the top right area of the keyboard	Used in combination with the ALT key to copy what is on the screen; you can then paste what you copied into a document or e-

The Key	Where its Typically Located	What the Key Does
		mail; hold the ALT key while pressing the PRINT SCREEN key
SCROLL LOCK Key	Usually located on right side of the keyboard	Use this key to lock scrolling of the page you are currently on. Press it again to unlock or stop scrolling.
SHIFT Key	There are usually 2 shift keys, one on each side of the keyboard; these keys may be labeled "shift" with an up arrow or simply have an up arrow on each key	Capitalizes a letter key when pressed and held while pressing the letter key; also executes the top function on a key when there are 2 functions shown on the key. Hold the key while pressing the next key in all cases
SPACE BAR	This is usually the longest key – it is more of a bar located in the center toward the bottom of the keyboard.	It creates a space when typing
TAB Key	Usually located at the top left of the keyboard	Will cause the cursor to jump to the next tabbed location (tabbed locations are preset or set by you)

The Key	Where its Typically Located	What the Key Does
TOUCH PAD	This is usually only found on a laptop and is located at the bottom center of the keyboard	Using your index finger, touch and your finger on the pad to move the cursor or pointer on the screen to a new location. You can also tap the screen to select a location on your screen; also, moving your finger vertically up and down on the right edge of the pad will cause your page to scroll. Note that with some computer operating systems, you would use two fingers on your touch pad to scroll up and down a page.

- **The Tower (desktop computer only)**

The tower is the large box that was described earlier as one of the major components of the desktop computer. The illustrative image

here is the same image provided earlier in this book that described the major components of a desktop computer. The image is shown again here since the tower is pointed out in the image. This section provides you more information regarding what the tower is and its purpose.

The tower is a box that holds the computer's "motherboard". The motherboard is what you could refer to as the "brains" of the computer. It has computer panels inside the box that holds the operating system and other hardware that allows the computer to run. The tower also holds most or all of the accessible and non-accessible computer drives. The accessible drives typically have doors that you can open to access the drives. The doors are located on the front of the tower. Accessible drives are described in more detail later in this section of the book.

Also on the front of the tower are connection points or ports that are frequently used by many computer users. These connection points or ports are also described later in this section of the book.

On the back of the tower are other connection points and ports that you do not need to access frequently. This is why these are located on the back of the tower. For example, the port to connect the Internet cable, which allows access the Internet, is on the back of the tower. A printer connection port is also usually located on the back of the tower. The tower should be located near your computer monitor and keyboard, however, it can sit on the floor.

- o **The Mouse and Touchpad**

The computer mouse is almost always used with a desktop computer and is optional for a laptop computer. It's optional for a laptop computer because laptops also have a "touch pad" that can do all the functions of a mouse. Along with the touch pad on some laptops are separate "mouse keys" that work similar to buttons on a mouse. Other laptop computers have the mouse key/button functions built into the touch pad. If you prefer to connect and use a mouse with a laptop, you can do so. The laptop keyboard image here shows the touch pad at the bottom center of the image along with two mouse buttons. These are described further in this section.

The mouse is similar in shape of a mouse (the animal) – that's where it gets its name (really). The cord coming from the mouse looks like the mouse's tail and the buttons on a mouse could resemble a mouse's eyes! The difference is that a computer mouse is more intelligent (thank goodness!). Cordless computer mice are also now available that work off wireless technology, however, wired and wireless mice are still both widely used today. You can get left-handed and right-handed computer mice.

The mouse is used for pointing and making selections on the screen, similar to the touch pad on a laptop. You move the mouse with your hand (or move your finger(s) on the touch pad) to move the cursor, or

26

your location, on the screen. The mouse and touch pad are very useful as they allow you to move around the screen very quickly.

When you click the left mouse button, it selects the location of the pointer on your screen. To make a selection on the screen with a touch pad, just tap the touch pad with your finger. When you click the right mouse button (on your mouse or computer), a pop-up menu of options appear on your screen. (On a laptop, if mouse button functions are build into the touch pad, then you may need to take other action to active right mouse button functions, e.g., use two fingers instead of one to click the mouse pad.) You can then select one of the options that appear in the pop-up box by using your mouse or touch pad by clicking on an option.

- ○ **Computer Drives**

Whether you have a desktop or laptop computer, you have drives working inside the computer that are contained (e.g., hard drives that you cannot easily access) and some drives that have 'drive doors' that you can access, such as CD/DVD drives.

CD/DVD drives are typically located on the separate tower for a desktop computer and on one side or the front edge on a laptop computer. You should be able to push the button on an accessible drive door to open it. Typically, when you insert a disk (CD or DVD) in a drive door, the drive will begin running (which you should be able to hear) and will start the program, the movie, or whatever is on the disk, CD, or DVD that you inserted.

Some drives can accept a CD or a DVD or both. Typically, it will say on the drive door if the drive is a CD drive, a DVD drive, or a CD and DVD drive. CD/DVD drives are either drives that can read CD/DVDs or are "read/write" drives, meaning you can read the CD/DVD placed in the drive and you can also write on the CD/DVD (if it is not protected to prevent erasing or writing).

- **Computer ports**

  o **USB ports**

  A 'port' is a connection point on your computer. Ports are where you plug something into them, typically another device (an accessory to the computer like a printer or a digital camera). USB ports refer to the type of ports they are and the connector it will accept. USB ports accept USB cords to be connected to them. USB ports are rectangular and the USB cords have a rectangular connector. Many accessories that you may want to connect to your computer state that to connect your accessory, to use a USB cord. An example image is provided here of USB ports on a computer and what the USB connector typically looks like.

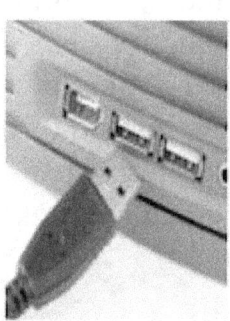

  USB Ports

  For example, if you want to view, edit, and/or save your pictures from a digital camera to your computer, you will typically connect your camera to your computer by connecting a USB cord (that is usually provided with your camera for this purpose). This is a reminder to use the manufacturer's documentation for your accessories to learn the proper way to connect accessories to your computer.

  o **Parallel and serial ports**

  Serial / Parallel Ports

  A parallel or serial port is typically used to connect a printer and some other accessories to your computer when the cord for the accessory has a parallel or serial connector cord that fits these ports. An example image is provided here of these types of connection ports. Again, use the manufacturer's documentation for your accessory to learn the proper way to connect it to your computer.

o **Telephone line port**

This port, or connection point, looks like a standard telephone connection that you might see for a telephone wall jack. You probably won't use this port if you purchased a high-speed Internet connection through the telephone company, TV cable provider, satellite or other provider. There is another port usually right next to it that looks just like it but it's a little wider. I talk about the network port next.

o **Network cable port**

This port looks like a telephone line connection point except it's a little larger. This is where you connect a network cable to give you access to a network of computers. This port has other purposes as well that will not be covered in detail in this book.

• **External speakers & headset connection**

You usually will also have a place to connect external speakers or a headset to the computer. While your computer has speakers built in, you can also connect external speakers to a desktop or laptop computer. Depending upon the quality of your internal speakers, you don't specifically need external speakers. External speakers are also inconvenient for laptop computers since you typically use a laptop in various locations and perhaps away from home.

Computer Speakers

Again, refer to the manufacturers' quick start guide(s) or manual for setup of any computer hardware or components.

- **Power connection**

Of course, to, there is the power connection and cord. Whether you have a desktop or laptop, you will use the power cord. All computers have batteries in them. However, the desktop computer is not meant to run on the battery alone. It needs the external power as well. A laptop can run for several hours on its fully charged battery – it's intended to do this. This is one of the reasons people generally like laptops. If your laptop computer has sufficient battery life, you can disconnect from external power and work on your laptop anywhere. Just plug the computer in when the battery gets low – you have a battery indicator in the right-hand corner of the screen for most PCs (top right-hand corner for most Mac computers) that tells you what the battery strength currently is when your computer is powered by battery. For PCs, a power cord plug is typically visible in the same location when your computer is receiving power via a power cord.

- **Other ports or connection points on a computer**

You will see other ports or connection points on your desktop tower, on the monitor, or on the keyboard. You will also see these on the sides, the front, or back edge of a laptop computer. These are other special connector ports that you may never use. The image here shows a laptop computer with the ports discussed earlier and ports that serve other purposes as well. Again, refer to your owner's manual or documentation for your computer, and for the accessory you want to connect to your computer, for more information.

➤ Turning the computer on and off

The computer is all hooked up. How do you turn it on and off? We will keep referring you to the manufacturers' documentation for your computer. That is the case here as well. There is a normal procedure for turning on and turning off your computer that is specific to your computer model. It is always recommended to use the manufacturer's recommended startup and shutdown procedure to turn your computer on and off. Doing so will help keep your computer stable and working properly. Sometimes computers don't respond as intended. The manufacturer documentation also typically provides procedures to use in these cases as well.

Power Button

Note: The power button is typically used to turn the computer on when it is off. The power button is not typically used to shut a computer off – programs needs to be closed then use the normal shut down process recommended in the manufacturer documentation for your computer.

Note: Many of the computer and computer program manufacturers are providing less written documentation with computers and providing more of the documentation on their web sites on the Internet. Typically, you will have sufficient written documentation provided with your new computer to unpack, setup, and install programs on your computer. Don't be too concerned with this as there is considerably more information online than you will need. Some manufacturers, however, still allow you to order complete written manuals and other documentation regarding your computer and programs if you are more comfortable having this documentation in hand. You can also save to your computer, or print help files and many manuals that you find online. You also typically have telephone support for a period of time after purchasing your computer.

Lesson 4

Getting an Internet Connection

➢   **How do I get an Internet connection?**

Basically, to connect to the World Wide Web ("WWW"), also referred to as the Internet, you will need an Internet connection for your computer. Third-party companies provide this service. So first, if you don't already have an  Internet provider and connection to the Internet, then you will want to find an Internet service provider. Otherwise, you can skip this section.

Internet service providers are typically a telecommunications company, a satellite provider, or a cable TV company that services your area. It's recommended that you find a service provider that can provide you with a "high-speed" connection. In this case, call them and tell them you want a "high-speed Internet connection." They may need to schedule an appointment with you to install a cable that comes into your home.

When the installer comes, they should test the Internet connection for you after they install the cable. It's suggested that you already have and set up your computer, have it turned on when the installer comes to your home. He/she 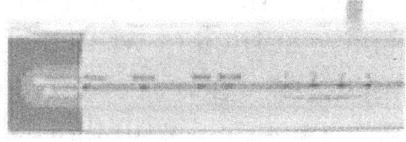 will usually hook up the wireless router for you as well if you have one.

The wireless router is only needed if you have more than one computer in your home or a laptop so you can use your computer(s) in more locations in your home instead of only the room the cable is installed. Before the installer leaves, he/she should have tested it, by connecting to the Internet to ensure it works properly. Be sure to ask the installer for a technical support customer service number in the event you ever lose your Internet connection.

A connection problem isn't always on their end, but your provider of the Internet connection will typically troubleshoot with you over the phone to fix your connection problem. If this happens to you, just call the technical support telephone number provided to you and tell them you lost your

Internet connection. If you can't bring up a web site that browses the Internet, like at www.google.com or www.yahoo.com, and instead, you receive an error page that says check your Internet connection, then you know you lost your connection. This usually doesn't happen often. However today, most Internet connections are usually very reliable.

A note about "dial-up" Internet connection: You can also buy a dial-up connection to the Internet. We don't advise using this unless this is the only option available to you. Where you live will dictate what your connection options are. A dial-up connection uses your telephone line, you are usually charged by the minute while you are using the Internet using dial-up (for the time that you are actually on the Internet) and is typically much slower that other connection types.

Lesson 5

Internet Security

➤ Security on the Internet

Before you connect to the Internet and start using it, let's talk for awhile about safety. Safety on the Internet generally refers to protecting your identity and information that is on your computer, relayed across communication lines, and provided to third-parties online.

• Anti-virus and other Internet security programs

When you first get your computer, typically it will be pre-loaded with a program to provide you with the online safety that will help lower the risk of using the Internet (and/or there will be an offer to purchase one of these programs). These programs are typically called "anti-virus" and Internet security programs. Anti-virus programs are intended to intercept external computer viruses before they infect or otherwise damage your computer or computer programs and provide levels of security to protect your personal files and information.

 Viruses can make your computer or its programs "sick" so that they don't work correctly. People who have the intent of doing this damage typically cause viruses. People with such ill intent have been referred to as computer "hackers". When you connect to the Internet you are connecting to the outside world and you can become electronically vulnerable to viruses and other actions of hackers. Anti-virus programs will help project you from viruses. You will also want to keep your anti-virus and other security programs on your computer up-to-date since new viruses are always a threat. Companies that make anti-virus and other computer security programs are consistently updating their programs, and making the updates available to you, to reduce your risk when using the Internet.

Note: It is not recommended that you automatically install a third-party anti-virus or other Internet security program on your computer without reading the manufacturer's documentation for your computer. The reason for this is that some computers come pre-loaded with very robust anti-virus and other Internet security programs. Installing other such programs from third-parties may interfere with the pre-installed programs. Companies that sell anti-virus programs also have programs to provide additional Internet security. If you aren't sure what to do after reading your computer manufacturer documentation, it is recommended that you contact the manufacturer of your computer.

- **Security of Web Pages**

  A web site can have secure pages and unsecure pages. That's fine and should not be a concern to you. This section explains when you should take the time to determine if a web page is secure. You will want to be concerned whether a web page is secure if you want to enter personal information on a web page such as a credit card number, a social security number, or other private or financial information.

  It is typical that web pages that do not require you to enter personal information are unsecure web pages. However, if you are on a web page where you will be entering personal information, that you want to keep personal, then you want the web page to be secure. When a web page is secure, your information is encrypted before it is transmitted. Encrypted refers to data being converted to unreadable data for transmission purposes. Here are things you can do to see if a web page is secure.

  1. You can check the address field of the page. Look for a "https" at the beginning of the web address for that page. Note the "s" at the end of the "https", which indicates the page is secure. If it says only "http" then the web page is not secure.

2. Another indication that a web page is secure is that an image of a padlock will appear in the menu bar or along the bottom of the frame of the window. You may be able to click on the lock and learn more information regarding the security of the site.

3. The image here shows the word "secure" next to the web address. A secure site may or may not show this word but it is another indication that the web page is secure.

4. Some web pages that are secure will sometimes have the security symbol on their page from the security company that secures their web page for them. There has been a lot of security effort put into protecting these images to prevent someone from copying these images.

- **Email attachments**

Another step that you can take to protect your computer when online is related to using e-mail. If you use e-mail, one important thing you can do is not open attachments to e-mail if you do not know who the e-mail is from. Sometimes attachments can contain viruses that begin to run on your computer when you open the attachment.

- **Common sense**

In general, use common sense to protect your personal information when you are online. For example, if you don't know the company that is trying  to sell you something online, understand that your risk increases when you provide your credit card or other personal information on these web sites. You will learn, in time, trusted web sites online.

- **Things that can go wrong**

If you get a virus in your computer, it can do a variety of things from causing very minor problems related to how your computer functions, up to erase and lock up your entire computer system. If your personal information is stolen, it can cause personal identify theft issues.

- **Keep it in perspective**

Don't be overly concerned with viruses and personal security online that it  prevents you from going online. Most people don't have serious problems with viruses and Internet security issues and you likely won't either. It is recommended, however, that you do follow through with the recommendations of your computer manufacturer and other experts to protect your computer and your personal information when online. Taking anti-virus and other steps recommended in this book will help to protect you online.

Lesson 6

Going Online!
How to Use the Internet

> ➢ **Start with browsing the Internet**

If you have not already read the section earlier in this book captioned "Internet Security" then you should do so now.

You are now ready to go online (that's what most people call it when they are getting on the Internet). It's recommended that you start with 'browsing' the Internet. This means just play  around with it to get a feel how to move around and find things on the Internet. The more you experience the Internet, the more comfortable you will become with it.

How do you browse the Internet? Let's get started. Here are steps to begin browsing the Internet.

1. You will have to have already purchased and connected to your computer an Internet connection as described earlier in this book.

2. Turn your computer on by pressing and releasing the power button on your laptop keyboard. If you are using a  desktop computer, the power button is typically located on your tower. The power button in both cases will typically illuminate when pressed, indicating your computer power is on.

    Your computer should then begin the startup process, also known as the "boot up" process. Before attempting to do anything else on your computer, let the computer complete the startup process after you turn it on – this should take less than a minute in most cases.

Don't be concerned if it takes a couple minutes. You can tell if the computer is still processing startup if you see a small hourglass (or some other indication that your computer is working) on your screen. Wait for the hourglass or other moving icon to disappear. When the computer is completely booted up, you can begin using it.

You should now see what is called your "desktop" or main screen of your computer. This view will likely have several small pictures (called icons) that represent programs on your computer. These icons are shortcuts to some (but not all) of the software programs currently stored on your computer. (The icons could also represent a link to an application that you can purchase or may be an advertisement.) On some computers, many of your programs will be shown in icons along the bottom or one of the sides of the screen.

You want to find the icon for your web browser program. This is the program that allows you to browse the Internet.

3. Several companies make web browsers. A couple of the most popular today are Internet Explorer® (a browser by Microsoft®) and Firefox® (a browser by Mozilla®). Google also makes a browser. On a Mac, the current browser is called Safari®. Look for one of these icons on your desktop (or refer to the documentation for your computer). Typically, your documentation will tell you what browser(s) are already pre-installed on your computer. The icons have names, so you should be able to find your browser program by looking for one of the browser names.

4. Point your pointer at the browser icon by using your mouse or touch pad. Put your pointer right over the icon. Click (sometimes a double click may be required) to open the browser program that you are pointing at with your pointer. This takes practice but after a couple of times of doing this, you will have this down in no time!

5.   The browser program installed on your computer should open in a new window. There could be a variety of information and advertisements on the window that opens. This is the start or "home" page of the program. (You can change later what page that you want to open when you open your browser.) We are now going to tell you the easiest way to browse the Internet.

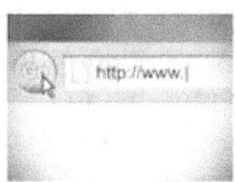

6.   There should be a box that is called an "address field" at the top of your open browser window. Next, you will be typing text in the address field or box. To do this, place your pointer in the address field box and click once with your left mouse button (or on a laptop, point at the box and touch your touch pad quickly). You should then see a blinking line in the address field box. You are now ready to type in the address field. Next, we will be typing a web site address that will take us to a search engine that allows you to search the Internet.

- **The search page**

7.   Here is how to get to a search page that allows you to browse the Internet. Type the following in the address field box:

www.google.com

You do not need to type the underline but you do need to type the periods in the address.

8.   Now hit your ENTER key. This will take you to Google's main page. Google® is what is called a search engine that is used to browse the Internet and many other things that you will learn later. Google has a search field in the middle of the screen that is very easy to see and

use. This is where you will enter text that tells the browser what you want to search the Internet for. (There are also other search engines like www.yahoo.com or www.ask.com.)

9. Look for the 'search field' on Google's home page. A search field looks like a box that is empty and may say "search" or something similar next to it. See the image here what a search field may look like. Google's search box may not look just like this one. The search field is typically at the top or middle of the screen. It usually very visible. Find the search field. This is where you will type something that you want to search for.

10. Put your cursor in the search field. How do you do that? By moving your mouse with your hand (or by moving your index  finger around on your touch pad) which will cause your pointer on the screen to move. Simply move the pointer on the screen until it is pointing inside of the search box. Then click your left mouse button (or tap your touch pad). Just one click (or tap) is enough. When you see a blinking line in the box, you are ready to enter some text.

- **Search terms**

11. Now type anything that you want to try searching for. To do this, you will enter "search terms" in the search field. For example, type the word "vacation" (don't type the parenthesis) in the search field box. ("Vacation" is your search term in this case.) If you make a mistake typing in the search field, that's okay. Hit the BACKSPACE or DELETE key on your keyboard. Every time you hit the BACKSPACE or DELETE key, it deletes one character. If you hold down this key, it will keep deleting until you release it or there is nothing more to delete. (You may need to use the ARROW keys on your keyboard to move your cursor to the right place in the search field to begin deleting text.)

12. After you have typed the word "vacation" in the search field, press the ENTER key on your keyboard. Pressing the enter key executes the search. You can also execute the search by clicking on the "search" or "go" button next to the search field on your screen.

13. Congratulations! You have just completed your first Internet search! The results of your search will appear on the screen. These search results are only the first page of all the results that your search located that corresponds to the word "vacation." When typing in one general word like "vacation", you will literally receive thousands or millions (yes, millions!) of hits. "Hits" is a common term that means results of your search.

You will be able to narrow your results or hits considerably when you type a string of words in the search field, which is what people typically do. An example would be to use the search words "vacation travel sites" or if you know you are looking for travel deals to Cancun you can type "travel deals to Cancun" or "Cancun deals" or something similar. Now is a good time to narrow your search so your hits will be more relevant to what you are searching for.

- **Search results**

14. Next, you will see your new list of search results. What should you do next? Anything that is underlined in the list is a "link" to a web site that matches your search terms. There are short descriptions of each hit that you received. The higher up on the list the link is located, the closer a match it is to your search terms. Look down through the list of search results and click on one of the links that interest you.

15. As mentioned earlier, all of your search results are typically too numerous to show on one page, so you will notice at the bottom of

the page that there are links to your other search results pages that match your search. If you want to look at your hits on these other pages, go to the bottom of the page and you will see something similar to the image here:

1 2 3 4 5 6 7 8 9 10 Next

These numbers are links to other pages that match your search terms.

Typically all links to other pages are underlined. This is so you can easily see where to click to open a web site that you are interested in.

- **Viewing search results**

16. When you click on a linked search hit, the web site associated with the link will open. The web site could belong to an individual, a company, a government site, or perhaps a non-profit organization that could be located anywhere in the world!

    When web pages open, continue to click on links or linked photos to move around the Internet. Yes, it's that easy!

    If the web site is not what you were looking for, then you can go back to the list of your search results that is covered next.

- **Go back to where you were**

17. Do you want to go back to where you were? For example, you clicked on a link and it's not what you are looking for. What do you  do? Hit the BACK button on the screen. It looks like an arrow pointing to the left and usually is located in the top left corner of the window that you currently have open. If you click on it once, it will take you back one page.

Every time you click it, it will take you back another page. Try going back to search results and click on the back button one time. You should be at your list of search results again.

- **Go forward again**

    18.   What if you want to go forward again to the very same location you were at? Click on the FORWARD button. It's an arrow pointing to the right and is usually located next to the BACK button. This should take you forward to where you were before you went back several pages. You can click it until you return to where you were. If the BACK or FORWARD buttons are grayed out, then you can't go in that direction any further.

- **I'm lost and want to start over!**

What if you get lost and want to start over with your Internet browsing or close one or more pages? There are a couple of things you can do. You can go back to the address field at the top of the browser window that is open and type www.google.com again. Doing this will take you back to the home page of Google where you started your first search. Now you can search for the same thing or start a new search by entering text in the search field. You can also enter a different web address in the address field.

If you are still lost, see the "X" in the top right or left corner of your open window? Click on it once. This will close the current window or page that you have open.

Keep closing windows! If you close a window and still see other open windows and you want to close them, just keep

clicking on the "X" in the top right or left corner of each open window. You will eventually return to your desktop (where your program icons located) when you have closed or minimized everything. (Minimized is discussed later in this section.)

Some computer operating systems require you to click on the name of an open program in the top left corner of your screen then click "close" or "quit" to close the open program. This is because these operating systems may have closed your open windows within a program (by clicking on the "X" in an open window) but it has not closed the program yet. If you close on "close" or "quit" under "FILE" on the menu, it may close the open document or window OR it may close the program, depending on the operating system that your computer uses.

- **A note about "active" windows**

You can have more than one window or program open at a time. This is really a convenient feature of computers. You can be working on writing a letter in a word processing program. Then you might decide that you want to research something on the Internet so you open your web browser. You can do this without closing the word processing program. You can also have several web browser windows open. However, unrelated to how many programs or windows that you may have open, you only have one "active" window at a time. The active window is the window that you are currently using. If you click on one of the other open windows, then that window becomes active and you can use that program or window. To make a window active, just click anywhere on the open window.

- **Making windows larger or smaller**

You may want to move an open window out of the way without closing it. You may notice that next to the "X" in the top left or right corner of the active window (that we discussed in the last section) are two other boxes or circles. These boxes or circles are used to minimize (make the active window smaller and move it out the way) or maximize the active window (to make the window larger).

Note: There is also another way to make open windows larger or smaller. You can do this by "dragging" the edges or the bottom right corner of the window. All operating systems do not do this exactly in the same way. However, if you see a triangle in the bottom right hand corner of your open window, the click and hold down your left mouse button or your touch pad while pointing at the triangle then drag the window edge. The window should get larger or smaller, depending on which way you drag the corner. As mentioned, some operating systems allow you to also select the edges of a open window and drag the edges in a similar way. In this case, you know that you have your pointer in the right place before beginning to drag when the pointer turns into a double arrow (a line with an arrow on each end of the line).

➢   **Other Internet Browsing Examples and Tips**

- **Go directly to a web site without searching for it**

    If you don't already have your browser program open, do so now.

    Do you remember how to do this? Do you recall that on your main desktop page where all those icons are? You are looking for Internet Explorer, Firefox, Safari or another web browser that you use. Click on your web browser. (Recall that on a PC, you may need to double click on program icons twice quickly to open them.) Now your browser should be open.

    Now you are ready to do another Internet search or you can go directly to a web site without having to search for it in Google.

    Do you remember the box at the top of your open browser window? Look for it now. You will remembers that this box is called the

'address field.' The important thing is that you know that this address field at the top of your screen in your browser program is where you put the names of web pages that you want to go to. Last time you used the address field, you typed in www.google.com. This time, we don't need to go to a search engine like Google. This is because this time we know what web site that we want to go to.

For example, if you want to find the Charles Schwab® web site, its easier to go directly to their site instead of searching for it by browsing. While you can find Charles Schwab online by searching for it, let's discuss how to go directly to it. Charles Schwab's web site address is as follows:

www.charlesschwab.com

When you know the web address you want to go to, you simply type it in the address field. Then hit the enter key which executes your command. The home page of the web site for Charles Schwab should open.

So, in review, there are 2 ways to go to web sites in a web browser:

1.   You can use a search engine like Google or Yahoo or Ask. To do this type one of these in the address field:

   - www.google.com
   - www.yahoo.com
   - www.ask.com

   Then you will use the "search" box to type text related to your search, then hit the ENTER key to execute your search.

   OR

2.   If you know the web address of the web site that you want to visit, then type the address in the address field of the open browser window and hit the ENTER key.

Let's try this again. For this example, let's assume that you heard that a company online named Amazon has the best prices for many products but you do not know their web address. Can you guess at the web address by typing what you think the web address may be in the address field? Yes you can. You may not always get the right web site to come up, but many times it does. So, let's try to find Amazon online.

Type the following address in the address field of your Internet browser program:

www.amazon.com

Now hit the ENTER key.

Waa-lah! You found the web site for Amazon.

Here is another example (practice makes perfect, right?) You may have heard in a television ad to visit a web site for more information that you want to obtain. The web address for the company is provided in the advertisement. They will say something with a ".com" after it typically, like basspro.com, walmart.com, bestbuy.com, walgreens.com, and so forth.

If you here such web addresses, simply put a "www." in front of the addresses when entering them into a browser address field. For example:

Walmart.com is entered into an address field as www.walmart.com

Bestbuy.com is entered into an address field as www.bestbuy.com

Walgreens.com is entered into an address field as www.walgreens.com

You will recall that typically capital letters or small letters will work the same way when entering web addresses in address fields. You cannot, however, have any spaces in a web address when entering an address in an address field. You do need to type the periods.

You can always browse to find the web site or information you are looking for as described earlier.

If you went to some of the above sites, you are experiencing going to web sites where you can shop online. However, let's go into more detail regarding shopping on the Internet in the next section.

➢ Shopping Online

• Searching online shopping sites

Shopping online is fun and so much more convenient that shopping at the mall! It probably also saves money by not jumping in your vehicle and driving somewhere to shop – and it's a timesaver to shop online!

Note: As a reminder, if you have not already read the section earlier in this book captioned "Internet Security" then you should do so now.

If you buy a product or service online, the tips in that section of the book will help you protect your personal information such as your credit card numbers. You do have options in most cases when shopping on the Internet to buy without using your credit card online. While security of using credit cards and providing other personal information on the Internet has greatly improved in recent years, you should take steps as recommended in your computer manufacturer documentation and in this book to provide yourself added security.

How do you shop online? Use the same process to browse the Internet that you learned earlier in this section of the book.

Here is an example of how to shop online. Say that you know that you want to learn more about or buy a tent that you saw in the Bass Pro Shops catalog or in one of their stores. In this case, you can open your browser program and type the following into the address field at the top of your browser window:

www.basspro.com

Then hit the ENTER key on your keyboard. This will open the Bass Pro Shop's web site. You should be at their home page (beginning page) of their web site.

Next, you will search for your tent on Bass Pro's home page by using their "search" field. This is the box next to the words "search for" on their home page. To do this, put your cursor in the search box. You will need to click your mouse or touch your touch pad with the pointer in the field so the pointer changes to a blinking line. This tells you that you can now type text (search terms) in the search box.

Next, type the following word in the search box:

tents

Now hit the ENTER key on your keyboard. This will take you to the first page of tents that Bass Pro has on their web site for sale.
Here is another example. What if you wanted to see all tents on sale from many sellers. In this case, open your web browser and in the search field at the top of your window (instead of on a specific store's web site), type the following:

tents on sale

Now hit the ENTER key on your keyboard. This will give you a list of "hits" in response to your search that were found. Some web sites may be retail stores. Some links that you click on in your search results may be individuals selling tents. Look at the web site addresses in your search results for quick information about the web site associated with each search result.

If you click on links in your search results, and its not what you are looking for or you want to search further, don't forget that you can just his your BACK button in the top left corner of your screen when browsing the Internet. The back button is the picture of the left arrow key in most cases. Just click on it with your mouse.

Also don't forget that if you are using a touch pad instead of a mouse, that you simply tap the touch pad once or twice to select something. This works the same as clicking the left mouse button.

- **Buy something online**

Let's assume that you found a tent that you would like to buy from BassPro Shops web site. Please know that every web site that sells products and services have a different process that customers must complete to purchase something from them online. The good news is that online purchase processes are more similar than they are different from one web site to another. The general process to purchase something online is covered here. Keep in mind, that as described, the process may be slightly different for each web site.

  o When you decide that the product or service that you are viewing is something that you want to purchase, you can simply click on the "shopping cart" or the words "add to shopping cart". The web page may instead have a button that says "buy now" that you would click on to add it to the shopping cart. The shopping cart is typically an icon or small image that looks like a shopping cart. Doing this adds what you were viewing to the shopping cart of the web site. You are not committed to purchase at this point. You can continue shopping or you can view your shopping cart.

  Note: There may be other questions that you need to answer before adding something to a shopping cart. If you select "add to shopping cart" too early, the web site will probably direct you back to the questions that you need to answer before you can continue. An example is if you are buying clothes, you may need to select quantity, size, and color.

  o If you want to view your shopping cart, there will be an option that states "view your shopping cart" that you would click on OR just click on the shopping cart icon to view what is in your cart. Your shopping cart should now be open and you should be able to see what you added to your shopping cart. If you change your mind, there is usually the option next to each item in your cart to delete one or more items. If you click on "delete" or "remove from my cart" or the "X" next to any item in your cart, it should be removed from your cart. There should also be an option when in your shopping cart to "continue shopping" if you aren't ready to "check out" yet.

o Let's assume you continued to shop at BassPro Shops online and you added several products that you believe you want to purchase to your shopping cart on their web site. You are now ready to stop shopping and "check out." To do this, click on "check out" or click on the shopping cart image. This should return you to your shopping cart page.

o Review the items in your shopping cart. Check that the items are correct along with the prices, quantities and other options listed for each item.

o Delete any items in the cart that you no longer want to purchase or make other necessary changes by following the directions on the screen.

o When everything in your cart is correct, click on "check out now" or "continue" or it may say "next".

o You are typically then taken to a web page that requests how you want the product shipped (if this hasn't already been covered). You typically have several shipment options. Make your shipment selection by clicking next to it. Then go to the next step as described above.

o A page should appear that requests your payment information. This is where you decide how you will pay for your purchases. If you are paying by credit card, the site will request your credit card information on this page. After you complete your purchase information and click to go to the next step, your card or bank information will be processed.

Note: Once you enter your credit card or bank information, you can assume that when you go to the next step, that you will be making the purchase. The site may or may not allow you another opportunity to confirm your purchases again before it processes your card or bank information.

Note: You should receive a confirmation page that states your transaction is complete. This tells you that the transaction completed successfully. If you provided an e-mail address to this company (either previously or during the checkout process), a confirmation of your purchase transaction is typically sent to you via e-mail.

Your purchase is now complete!

- **Customer Service of Companies Online**

Customer service online is similar to customer service offline. In other words, there are all kinds when it comes to customer service. The same applies to return policies, shipment problems, and more. It's a good idea to do business online with companies that you know and trust since you will be providing them with your credit card and other personal information.

➢ **E-Mail**

- **What is e-mail and what can I do with it**

This book is not intended to go into depth regarding how to use e-mail as all e-mail is not alike. Instead, we tell you here what you can use an e-mail for and where to get an e-mail account. E-mail providers mentioned in this book provide robust help files online that tell you how to you their e-mail programs that you can review, if needed, after you sign up for an e-mail account.

There are many benefits to using e-mail. Using e-mail is exciting because you can stay more closely in touch with your family and friends. E-mail hasn't replaced phone calls when you need or want to connect via phone, but it has replaced some phone communications because it's free, a less obtrusive way to connect, easy, and it's convenient. E-mail, and other online communications, such as "texting" and other social networking that is occurring online is where people are communicating today. So, go ahead! Come on board and find out what people, including your family and friends, are communicating about online!

Here is a list of advantages of using e-mail and other online communication tools – the nice part about e-mail is all of the following is optional and can be customized by you to meet your needs:

- Communicate with family and friends
- Receive written confirmation of online payments of bills
- Receive written confirmation of appointments made online (and some appointments not made online!)
- Be notified when sales happen at your favorite stores
- Be notified when special airline rates or packages are offered to your favorite destinations
- Receive written confirmation of booked travel
- Be notified when certain events occur with your credit cards (e.g., a charge is made to your card, your balance exceeds a dollar amount you indicate, etc.)
- Be notified when your checking, savings, or investment account reaches a dollar amount you indicate
- Conduct customer service communications with companies (this is very convenient compared to calling companies to manage this)
- Check and read your e-mail communications at your convenience
- And much more than can be listed here!

- **Getting an e-mail account**

The first rule of thumb is not to pay for an e-mail account. While some companies used to charge for this, most e-mail accounts are free today. There are companies that there are 'no strings attached' when setting up an e-mail account with them. It's suggested that you set up an e-mail account with one of the larger e-mail account providers. This is because these companies have robust security associated with their e-mail applications. Examples are as follows:

- Google an www.google.com
  Google's e-mail program is called "Gmail". You can go to their web site as shown here and click on "gmail" and click on "set up an e-mail account". It's that easy but more information on how to do this follows in the next section of this book. It's free.

- Yahoo at www.yahoo.com
  Yahoo's e-mail program is known as "Yahoo Email". It's also easy to set up a new account and is also free.

  There are many more options to set up a free e-mail account. These are just a couple of examples. See the list of examples of where you can get a free e-mail account at the end of this book.

The How-To Glossary

You may not read this glossary word for word and instead use it as a reference as needed, but it provides a lot of useful information.

This glossary includes basic words that are helpful to know. These are not technical definitions but commonly used descriptions of the word and examples of the words.

Note: As always, the manufacturer documentation for your computer is the best resource for you and should be relied on in all cases.

Word	Description of the Word and How it is Used	Example of the Word
"App" or Application	"App" is an acronym for application that typically refers to a software application or program. These are programs that allow you to do different tasks on your computer.	Examples of computer applications are: • Microsoft Word® – word-processing software application to create and save word documents • Microsoft Excel® - a spreadsheet software application for calculations, graphs, charts • Online calendar application

Word	Description of the Word and How it is Used	Example of the Word
		• Email program or application
Bookmarks	Bookmarks help you mark a place on the Internet that you may want to visit at a later time.	If you have a favorite travel site, you can save it to your "favorites" or "bookmarks" by clicking on one of these words on the toolbar at the top of your browser window.
Browser	A web browser is a program used to search the Internet.	Examples of browsers are: Microsoft's Internet Explorer® Mozilla's Firefox®
Cyberspace	Cyberspace is a virtual location. You are in cyberspace when you are on the Internet.	
Cursor	The cursor is a visible indication of where you are located in an open window. The cursor changes to a blinking vertical line to indicate you are in a text field where text can be entered. An example is when you click inside of a web address field. If you don't see a blinking line, move your mouse to find your pointer on the screen. If you put the pointer in a text box then click the left mouse button, the pointer should change to a cursor.	
Emotional Expression in writing	These are characters that you can type that are informal ways to show emotion in writings, such	Here is an example: Type the following: :) Which is a colon and a right parentheses. When

Word	Description of the Word and How it is Used	Example of the Word
	as in an e-mail.	these two characters are used together, it means happy or smiling in written communications. If you look at these marks sideways, they look like faces. Try typing these symbols on your keyboard that represent the emotions indicated: :-) happy or smiling :D very happy :-{ sad ;) winking {:-{ worried :O surprised :-\ confused
Download	Download typically refers to when you move something from the Internet to your computer or to a CD.	Following are examples of what you can download from the Internet: • Your bank statement • Your tax return • A book • A software application or

Word	Description of the Word and How it is Used	Example of the Word
		program
E-mail	E-mail is electronic mail that is enabled by the Internet. Email is extremely fast, near instant in many cases. People may have multiple e-mail accounts for different purposes, e.g., work e-mail, one or more personal e-mail addresses. Today, phones and other handheld electronics also provide access to your e-mail accounts.	
File	If you have ever been to someone's office, you probably know what a file cabinet looks like. Inside the cabinet there are usually file folders, which hold information that the office workers have saved there so they can find it quickly later. A file on a computer is like a file in an office, and your computer is like the file cabinet. In a computer file, you can save anything from a letter you typed to a picture you found on the Internet or took on your camera.	
Hardware	Your computer is made of hard pieces of metal, plastic, and glass. Sometimes people will call your computer, or parts of your computer, "hardware." That doesn't mean that there is a hammer or nails inside your computer!	Examples of hardware are: Desktop Computer: Monitor Tower Keyboard Mouse Laptop Computer External Speakers for a computer Printer Web Cam

Word	Description of the Word and How it is Used	Example of the Word
Home page	Just as a personal is a place where someone lives, a personal page is a place where a people, groups, governments, organizations, and companies "live" on the World Wide Web. If you have a personal page on the Web, you can put fun pictures, sounds, and information on it. Other people can visit your personal page, look at the pictures, listen to the sounds, and read the information.	
Internet	The Internet is made up of computers all over the world. The computers are connected by phone lines or cables. They all share a common language and understand a set of Internet rules so they can relay information whenever you need it. You can use the Internet to send e-mail to a friend across the world, or watch a movie clip on your computer, or finish a personal work project about the solar system.	
Internet Service Provider	A company that helps you get your computer hooked up to the Internet is an Internet service provider. This company might give you an e-mail address so other people can send you mail on your computer.	
Links	Links are 'active' or 'hot' links. Clicking on links take you somewhere else, typically located on the Internet. It's a quick way to get around when on the Internet. So links are extensively used on the World Wide Web (the Web or Internet or Net) as shortcuts to other locations	An example of using links on a web site: You went to the web site www.charlesschwab.com because you want to check your investments with Charles Schwab.

Word	Description of the Word and How it is Used	Example of the Word
	or information on the Web. You click on links and a new page or window will open. What opens depends on what the link is linked to. Links are usually a different font color from other text on the page and is sometimes underlined. This is so you can find these links easily on a page. Pictures or icons or anything that you see on a page can be linked. You can also tell if something is linked by putting your cursor over something. If your pointer changes to a selection hand (looks like a hand with a finger pointing at the link), then what you are pointing on is linked. If you then click your left mouse button while hovering over the linked text or picture, it will activate the link and take you to the page or location to which the text or picture is linked.	
Modem	A modem lets you use your telephone to get on the Internet. Usually, a modem is a small box that sits between your computer and the telephone line coming into your house. It makes it possible for your phone line	

Word	Description of the Word and How it is Used	Example of the Word
	to send information instead of just sending your voice.	
Mouse	It's not really a mouse but more than one computer mouse is called mice! The mouse is called what it is because it's similar to the size and shape of a mouse! It's can be hooked up to desktop or laptop computers and can help you navigate on your screen. You will use the mouse to point to pictures or words and to select them by 'clicking' a button on the mouse. If you don't have a mouse, you do these functions using a touch pad or scroll ball but you usually only find these on laptops or smaller computers. Most people only use a mouse connected to their desktop computer, at personal or at work. Also see "touch pad" and "trackball" in this glossary. The mouse, the touch pad, and the trackball all help you move around on your screen. So do the keys with arrows on them. The mouse, the touch pad, and the trackball all do the same basic functions – allow you to move around the screen as needed. Most people don't use a mouse with a laptop – they use the touch pad. This is because you have to have a hard service to use the mouse. That's fine if you want to use a mouse with a laptop but you will likely soon fine the touch pad is easier to use with a laptop.	
Net	"The 'Net" is a nickname for the Internet. You might also hear or read about other names for the Internet: the Information Superhighway, the Infobahn, the I-way, and so on.	
Netiquette	Netiquette is the name for manners on the Internet. It refer to using the same rules of respect in communications online (on the Internet) and in communications such as in e-mails.	

Word	Description of the Word and How it is Used	Example of the Word
Network	When several computers are connected together, this makes a network. For example, if you visit your local library, you might find that the library has some computers that you can use to look for books. These library computers are probably connected to each other so they can share information.	
Online	"Online" is the time you spend working or playing on the Internet. "Offline" is the time when spend working on the computer that is not on the Internet. When you are using e-mail, for example, you are also online because the e-mail is sent via the Internet. If you are paying by the minute to be online to your Internet Provider, you likely have a "dial-up" connection. This can get expensive. If you have a high-speed connection through a TV cable company, phone or satellite company, you likely pay one flat monthly fee for the internet connection unrelated to usage – so even if you don't use it, you pay for it. There are variations of these plans with Internet providers at different costs.	
Search Engines	Once you have a browser open on your computer screen, you will want to use a search engine to search the Internet.	Examples of search engines are: Google at www.google.com Yahoo at www.yahoo.com MSN at www.microsoft.com America Online at www.aol.com

Word	Description of the Word and How it is Used	Example of the Word
		Also see the popular web site list at the end of this book.
Touch Pad	The touch pad is an optional way to move the pointer around on a screen instead of using the mouse or a trackball. Touch pads and trackballs are usually only on laptops and not desktop keyboards. This is because with a desktop, you typically have a mouse connected. The mouse, the touch pad, and the trackball all do the same basic functions – allows you to move around the screen as needed. Most people don't use a mouse with a laptop – they use the touch pad. This is because you have to have a hard surface to use the mouse for it to work properly. That's fine if you want to use a mouse with a laptop but you will likely soon fine the touch pad is easier to use with a laptop. Touch pad are usually located below the keyboard and is a square or rectangle "pad" that you touch, usually with your index finger and move your finger around. This moves the pointer or cursor on the screen. It helps you find the pointer or cursor because when you move it, it becomes visible. Using the touch pad is a quick way to move around the screen. Also see SELECTION keys in this glossary that talk about what those keys are on a laptop that are typically located just above and/or below, or otherwise adjacent to the touch pad. Tip: You can also use your touch pad to make	

Word	Description of the Word and How it is Used	Example of the Word
	selections instead of using the selection key. Just tap the touch pad with your finger. You may need to do it once or twice quickly.	
Trackball	The trackball is an optional way to move the pointer around on a screen instead of using the mouse or a touch pad. Touch pads and trackballs are usually only on laptops and not desktop keyboards. This is because with a desktop, you typically have a mouse connected. The mouse, the touch pad, and the trackball all do the same basic functions – they allow you to move around the screen as needed. Most people don't use a mouse with a laptop – they use the touch pad. This is because you have to have a hard surface to use the mouse for it to work properly. That's fine if you want to use a mouse with a laptop but you will likely soon fine the touch pad is easier to use with a laptop.	
Web Address	A web address is an address that refers to a web site. Examples are walmart.com or mojoey.com. The 'com' at the end of a web address stands for commercial, but it can be a retailer, other commercial business, or an individual that is not in business. It's the most commonly used extension in a web address. The other commonly used web address that you may want to know about end in '.edu' or '.org'. The first one (.edu) tells you it's a web site for an educational institution like colleges for example. The second one (.org) represent non-profit	

Word	Description of the Word and How it is Used	Example of the Word
	organizations. If you want to know if the website is related to a governmental entity or agency, its web address will end in .gov. You will also see web addresses that end in country abbreviations. Examples are '.uk' (for United Kingdom), '.au' (for Australia). These web sites typically represent a web site that is related to these countries, e.g., the owners of the site do business there. See the list of popular web sites with their web addresses at the end of this book.	
Web Cam	This is an easy one. It's a camera that works across the web (Internet). It's a piece of hardware that looks like an eye that usually sits on top of your monitor/display or is built into your computer that when used, shows your picture or whoever is in front of the camera. If someone you are communicating also has a web cam, then it allows you to see other when communicating.	
World Wide Web	The World Wide Web (WWW) is part of the Internet. On the Web, bits of information are linked together -- just like strands in a real spider web -- to make things easier to find. You can go anywhere on the Web just by clicking on a link, which is a shortcut to something on the Internet. That's why you see "www" in web addresses. Many people interchange the words "World Wide Web", the "Internet", the "web", and the "net" for short. The World Wide Web is represented in a web site address by "www".	

Troubleshooting Guide

Use this guide as a reference as needed throughout your learning journey. Most of the information in this guide is covered throughout the book, so you can also refer to the Table of Contents at the beginning of this book for more information.

Note: As always, the manufacturer documentation for your computer is the best resource for you and should be relied on in all cases. The information here is not meant to replace manufacturer-provided processes described here or in this book generally.

If This:	Then Do This:
How do I turn the computer on?	Press the computer power button. The computer power button is usually located at the top center of the keyboard on a laptop and on the hard drive on a desktop computer.
How do I turn the computer off?	This process is somewhat different for most computer operating systems. Refer to the manufacturer documentation for your computer. In most cases, you will not simply press the power button to shut down your computer without completing other processes first to properly shut down your computer.
What if I accidently delete or cut something that I did not intend to?	Don't worry. You can un-do most of what you do in computer programs in case you do something unintentionally. Just click the "un-do" on the menu bar at the top of the screen. The un-do option usually looks like a backward arrow on the menu bar – just click on it. Every time you click it, it will un-do the previous action and keeps un-doing consecutive actions executed every time you click it. If you un-do too much, just click the "re-do" that looks like a forward arrow.
How do I select something on the	If you are using a mouse, click the left mouse button. If you are using a touch pad, do a quick

If This:	Then Do This:
screen?	tap on the touch pad – you may need to tap the pad once or twice quickly
What is the right mouse button or right mouse key on a keyboard for?	Both of these do the same or similar functions. If you click on it, another menu of options appear. If you want to do something in the pop-up menu that appears, just click on it. The menu of options that will appear may depend on what you are doing when you click it.
How do I "cut" something and why would I need to?	Suppose you want to delete something. You can push the backspace key. You can push the delete key if your cursor is before what you want to delete. But what if you want to delete a lot of text? It will take quite a while to delete pages of text, for example, holding down the delete or backspace key. Instead, you can "select" the text you want to cut (delete) then press the right mouse button and select "cut". Don't worry. You can un-do most of what you do in computer programs in case you do something unintentionally. Just click the "un-do" button on the menu bar at the top of the screen.
How do I "copy and paste" or "cut and paste" something and why would I want to do this?	Copy and pasting prevents you having to re-type text and allows you to copy some pictures (if not protected from copying). When you "cut and paste" you are removing something from its current location, or moving it and placing it (pasting it) in a new location. Technically you can cut and paste in the same location too. Information and graphics owned by others may be protected from copying for copyright or trademark protection. You can copy and paste in different applications or online in some cases. This feature is very helpful when creating and editing a written document, like in the program Word®. You can move an entire paragraph or paragraphs or pages at one time very quickly.

If This:	Then Do This:
How do I "drag" something and why would I need to?	Sometimes you will receive instruction to select and drag something, either text or a picture or an icon for example, to another location. When you drag something, you are typically either moving or copying something to another location. File management uses this feature a lot. It's an easy way to move things around, like folders, and to get organized. How do you do it? If you want to drag something, select it with your touch pad or left selection key or left mouse button. Hold down the selection key or left mouse button while you move your pointer to the location that you want to move or copy whatever it is that you are dragging. When you have dragged it to the desired location, then release the key or mouse button.
How do I save a document?	Typically, in the program you are working in, click the word "File" then click "Save". The file management program will open in a pop-up menu. Select the location where you want to save the file, typically somewhere in the "my documents folder" then give your new file a name in the name field. Then click save. The file will save to one of your drives.
How do you use the menu bars in most programs and in your Internet Browser?	You typically have menu bars on the top and bottom of your screen and sometimes on the left and right sides of your screen in most programs and when online on the Internet. Menu bars include a group of little photos of pictures that are called "icons." If you hover over an icon with your pointer, usually a little pop-up window appears that tells you what the icon or menu item does if you were to click on it. These are short cuts to actions you may want to take. There is also a menu bar with words like "File, Edit, View, Insert, Format, Tools", etc. Click on these

If This:	Then Do This:
	to see the same or other menu options of things you can do in the program you are in. If the menu item is darkened then it is not an option to execute it based on where you are currently located in a program.

Popular Web Sites

Following these instructions is a list of some of the popular web sites at the time of publishing of this book. The web sites are grouped by subject.

Note: The author of this book does not personally endorse any of the companies represented in this web site list or guarantee safety of your personal information or computer when using one or more of these web sites.

You can do one of the following to go to one of the web sites listed in the last column of the list:

 1. If you are reading this on your computer, click on the web site name. Your browser should open the web site you click on; if that doesn't work (because the web site may no longer be linked in your document), do one of the other 2 options that follow:

2. Copy and paste the web site into a web address field in your browser. To do this, hold the left mouse button as you "select" the web site name; it will appear highlighted; click your right mouse button and select the "copy" option; open your web browser; place your cursor in the address field; click your right mouse button again; select "paste" from the option list; press enter on your computer keyboard; the web site should open.

3. Open your web browser; type the web site in the address field in your browser; press ENTER on your computer keyboard; the web site should open. Note: When typing web addresses, enter them exactly as provided in the last column of the following table without spaces; what may look like a space is an underline that looks like this with the quotation marks: "_".

Subject	Description	Web Site
Arts & Science	Links to web sites of the top-rated museums in the world	www.worldreviewer.com/travel-guides/specialist-museum/
Arts & Science	Links to the top-rated photographer web sites	http://www.topphotographers.com/
Arts & Science	U.S. National Gallery of Art	http://www.nga.gov/
Arts & Science	Smithsonian Museums	http://www.si.edu/museums/
Arts & Science	Space exploration, scientific discovery and aeronautics research	www.nasa.gov
Best-Rated Web Sites on the Internet	Links to top-rated web sites	http://www.worldbest.com/news_zines.htm
Consumer	The Consumerist	http://www.consumerist.com/
Consumer	Consumer Reports	www.consumerreports.org
Consumer	Listing of top-rated consumer web sites	www.bestconsumersites.com
Consumer	Best-rated online customer service contact information for	www.Gethuman.com

Subject	Description	Web Site
	companies	
Coupons	Online coupons	www.retailmenot.com
Coupons	Online coupons	www.coupons.com
Coupons	Online coupons	www.couponcabin.com
Coupons	Online coupons	www.couponmom.com
Coupons	Online coupons	www.smartsource.com
Credit Cards	Compare credit card offers	http://www.creditcards.com/
Education	Top university rankings	http://www.topuniversities.com/university-rankings
Education	Find schools to attend and degree information	http://www.geteducated.com/
Email	Top-rated free e-mail sites	http://e-mail.about.com/od/windowse-mailclients/tp/free_e-mail_prog.htm
Email	Google - free e-mail	www.google-mail.com
Encyclopedia Online	The encyclopedia that anyone can edit	www.wikipedia.com
Finances & Investment	Charles Schwab	www.charlesschwab.com
Finances &	Listing of top-rated	http://newrulesofinvesting

Subject	Description	Web Site
Investment	investment web sites	com/top-5-investment-sites
Finances & Investment / Government	U.S. government web site regarding money management	www.mymoney.gov
Finances & Investments	Yahoo! Finance	www.finance.yahoo.com
Games Online	Monopoly	http://board-games.pogo.com/games/monopoly
Games Online	Online board games	http://board-games.pogo.com/
Games Online	Online board and card games	http://boardgames.about.com/od/playgamesonline/Play_Games_Online.htm
Government – U.S., State, and Local	List of U.S. state and local government web sites and links	http://www.usa.gov/Agencies/State_and_Territories.shtml
Government – U.S.	List of all U.S. Federal web sites	http://www.usa.gov/Agencies/Federal/All_Agencies/index.shtml
Government – U.S. (also see other U.S. Government	U.S. main web site	www.usa.gov

Subject	Description	Web Site
web sites under other topics in this list)		
Government - Canada	List of Canada's government web addresses	www.canada.gc.ca/depts/major/depind-eng.html
Health	Mayo Clinic – health care, symptom, and drug information	www.mayoclinic.com
Health	WebMD – health care, symptom, and drug information	www.webmd.com
Health	25 of the most popular health web sites	http://www.ebizmba.com/articles/health-websites
Health	Best-rated online drug information	www.CRBestBuyDrugs.org
Health	Medline Plus - Guide to prescription and over-the-counter medications provided by the United States Pharmacopeia	http://www.nlm.nih.gov/medlineplus/druginformation.html
Health	U.S. Dept. of Health and Human Resources - Agency for	http://www.ahrq.gov

Subject	Description	Web Site
	Healthcare Research and Quality (AHRQ) projects, publications, and research related to *health* care for the *elderly*	
Health	Links to top-rated web sites for health and wellness for seniors	http://www.rncentral.com/nursing-library/careplans/top_100_health_and_wellness_sites_for_seniors
Humor / Comedy	Humor and senior citizens	http://seniors.lovetoknow.com/Senior_Citizens_Humor_Sites
Humor / Comedy	Clean jokes	www.cleanjoke.com
Humor - Comedy	Links to top-rated good clean jokes and humor	www.goodcleanjokes.com
Humor / Comedy	Clean comedians	http://www.cleancomedians.com/
Maps	Offers maps, satellite images for complex or pinpointed regional searches, topography and street views, etc.	www.earth.google.com

Subject	Description	Web Site
Maps	Find local businesses, view *maps* and get driving directions in Google *Maps, topography and street view*	www.maps.google.com
Maps	Driving directions and *maps*. See local traffic and road conditions, find nearby businesses and restaurants, plus explore street *maps*, etc.	www.mapquest.com
Maps	Locate nearly any place on Earth, and show street *maps*, satellite views, bird's eye views, and 3-D navigation	www.nationalgeographic.com or www.**map**redirect.national geographic.com/**map**machi ne/index.html
Maps	*Map store* - wall *maps*, travel *maps*, atlases, digital *maps*, etc.	www.maps.com
Maps	Get *online* driving directions you can trust from Rand McNally. Download *maps*, add multiple stops	www.randmcnally.com

Subject	Description	Web Site
	check real-time traffic updates, avoid road construction, etc.	
Money	Foreign exchange information	http://www.oanda.com/
Money	Currency converter	http://www.xe.com/ucc/
Money	Currency converter	http://www.x-rates.com/
Movies	Top-rated movies	http://movies.yahoo.com/mvc/top10
Music	iTunes	www.itunes.com
Music	eMusic	www.emusic.com
Music	Links to band and orchestra web sites	http://www.bassoon.org/orchestr.htm
Nature	Butterflies	http://butterflywebsite.com/
Nature	Top-rated bird web sites	http://www.birding.com/bestwebsites.asp
Networking Online	Facebook	www.facebook.com
Networking Online	YouTube	www.youtube.com
News & Politics	CNN	www.cnn.com
News &	MSNBC	www.msnbc.com

Subject	Description	Web Site
Politics		
News & Politics	CBS News	www.cbsnews.com
News & Politics	ABC News	www.abcnews.go.com
News & Politics	USA Today	www.usatoday.com
News & Politics	Wall Street Journal	www.wsj.com
News & Politics	The New York Times	www.nytimes.com
News & Politics	USA Today	www.usatoday.com
News & Politics	US News & World Report	www.usnews.com
News & Politics	Links to top-rated online newspapers	http://www.onlinenewspapers.com/Top50/Top50-CurrentUS.htm
Philanthropy	Best-rated charity watchdog online	www.CharityNavigator.org
Philanthropy	Listing of best-rated green philanthropy web sites	www.greatgreenlist.com
Real Estate	Most visited real estate web sites and links	http://www.realestateabc.com/top100/top100.asp

Subject	Description	Web Site
Retirement	AARP - a nonprofit, nonpartisan membership organization that helps people 50 and over	www.aarp.org
Retirement	Links to top-rated retirement web sites	http://seniorjournal.com/NEWS/Retirement/5-10-11RetirementWebsites.htm
Retirement	Links to top-rated retirement web sites	http://www.newretirement.com/Planning101/Retirement_Links.aspx
Retirement	Retirement living information	http://retirementliving.com/
Retirement	U.S. government web site regarding retirement	http://www.opm.gov/retire/index.aspx
Search Engine	Ask Geeves – Search engine site to search the Internet	www.ask.com
Search Engine	Google – Search engine site to search the Internet	www.google.com
Search Engine	Yahoo – Search engine site to search the Internet and Internet content provider	www.yahoo.com

Subject	Description	Web Site
Search Engine	Microsoft – Search engine site to search the Internet and Internet content provider	www.msn.com
Search Engine	America Online – Search engine site to search the Internet and Internet content provider	www.aol.com
Senior Citizens	Love to Know Seniors	http://seniors.lovetoknow.com
Senior Citizens	Links to top-rated web sites for senior citizens	http://www.internetseniorsuccess.com/seniorsites.htm
Senior Citizens	Links to top-rated web sites for senior citizens	http://www.suddenlysenior.com/links.shtml
Shopping	Links to top-rated online shopping sites	www.toponlineshopping.com
Shopping	Links to top-rated furniture web sites	http://www.furnituretopsites.com/
Shopping	Buy and sell handmade items	http://www.etsy.com/
Shopping	Buy and sell almost anything	www.ebay.com

Subject	Description	Web Site
Shopping	Buy and sell used and new books	www.amazon.com
Shopping	Books, general merchandise	www.amazon.com
Shopping	Fishing, hunting, camping	www.basspro.com
Shopping	Greeting cards, gifts	www.hallmark.com
Shopping	Pets and pet supply	www.petsmart.com
Shopping	Pharmacy and drug store supply	www.osco.com
Shopping	Pharmacy and drug store supply	www.walgreens.com
Shopping	General merchandise, pharmacy and drug store supply	www.walmart.com
Social Security	U.S. Social Security Administration	www.ssa.gov
Sports	ESPN	www.espn.go.com
Sports	Football	www.nfl.com
Sports	Top-rated fishing locations / web sites	http://www.topfishingsites.com/
Sports	Racing	www.nascar.com

Subject	Description	Web Site
Sports	Fox Sports	www.foxsports.com
Sports	Olympics	www.olympic.org
Sports	Special Olympics	www.specialolympics.org
Taxes	U.S. Internal Revenue Service (IRS)	www.irs.gov
Travel	Links to top-rated travel sites	http://www.consumersearch.com/travel-sites
Travel	U.S. Government – Current travel warnings	http://travel.state.gov/travel/cis_pa_tw/tw/tw_1764.html
Travel	U.S. Government State Dept. - Preparing for a trip abroad	http://www.state.gov/travel/
Travel	Check travel costs and book travel	www.orbitz.com
Travel	Check travel costs and book travel	www.cheaptickets.com
Travel	Check travel costs and book travel	www.expedia.com
Travel	Links to web sites of all airlines worldwide	http://www.oag.com/northamerica/airlineandairport/airlinedirectory6.asp
Travel	Links to web sites of all airlines in North America	http://www.kls2.com/airlines/n-america.html

Example Sources for Free Email Accounts

Note: The author of this book does not personally endorse any of the companies represented in this list or guarantee safety of your personal information or computer when using one or more of these services.

E-mail Provider	Comments	Go to Web Site
Google	Click on "Gmail" then "create an account"	www.google.com or www.gmail.com
Yahoo	Click on "new here? Sign up"	www.yahoo.com
Microsoft	Click on "sign up"	www.hotmail.com